WHY WON'T THEY PAY ME WHAT I'M WORTH?

Rodney Koop

Published by Best Seller Publishing®, Pasadena, CA

Best Seller Publishing® is a registered trademark

Printed in the United States of America.

ISBN-13: 978-1548509965

ISBN-10: 1548509965

This publication is designed to provide accurate and authoritative information with regard to the subject matter covered. It is sold with the understanding that the publisher is not engaged in rendering legal, accounting, or other professional advice. If legal advice or other expert assistance is required, the services of a competent professional should be sought. The opinions expressed by the authors in this book are not endorsed by Best Seller Publishing® and are the sole responsibility of the author rendering the opinion.

Most Best Seller Publishing® titles are available at special quantity discounts for bulk purchases for sales promotions, premiums, fundraising, and educational use. Special versions or book excerpts can also be created to fit specific needs.

For more information, please write:

Best Seller Publishing®

1346 Walnut Street, #205

Pasadena, CA 91106

or call 1(626) 765 9750

Toll Free: 1(844) 850-3500

Visit us online at: www.BestSellerPublishing.org

"Ok Rodney, we'll give it 6 more months."

– Karen Koop / wife of an entrepreneur.

TABLE OF CONTENTS

Preface... ix

Introduction 1

Chapter 1 Skilled Craftsmen—A Lifetime of Lessons 5

Chapter 2 The Law of Unintended Consequences........................11

Chapter 3 The Fantasy Ferris Wheel.................................19

Chapter 4 The Pool Just Got Smaller...............................25

Chapter 5 Tech Versus Salesman 31

Chapter 6 The Cloning Myth..41

Chapter 7 The Habitual Buyer 49

Chapter 8 Shoppers, Discounts, and Options 55

Chapter 9 The Solution..63

About the Author..73

It's always about price.
Until you make it about something else.

—Rodney Koop

PREFACE

Starting out as a contractor, the idea of owning my own company was an exciting endeavor. I had high hopes that I would soon be wealthy and happy. Being in charge of the books, the trucks, and the time had to be the dream of anyone who had worked for other people their entire life. I soon found out that running a contracting business took a lot more work than I had bargained for. For years, that "wealthy and happy" dream was just that, a dream. I was broke and discouraged.

Making payroll by Friday was almost impossible, and I hated being in business. In 1998, every Thursday around 6 p.m., when I had to transfer payroll from my bank account to the payroll company's bank account, I was secretly wishing that my business would somehow vanish into thin air. The roster showed the most employees I had ever staffed at one time up to that point, 18 to be exact. Baffled I thought, "How is it that a full staff can't pull together and find a way to make more money than the day before?" I was constantly spinning the ole' wheel of, "If I could just teach my techs to sell, then…" Well, we would inevitably be out of the woods, right?

Many contractors rely heavily on their techs' ability to sell in the home. If upsells and upgrades aren't happening, the business is usually doomed. Can you imagine being a technician and the weight of the business resting on your ability to snap out of "fix it" mode and into "you'd better sell more or we're going under" mode? All I wanted to do at 6 p.m. every Thursday was to transfer the $10,000 in payroll with no afterthought of business suicide. So I began to invest non-existent money into my technicians in hopes that they would save my company and learn how to be great salesmen. Lead a horse to water, and he'll drink, right? Well, not these horses.

After training seminars, videos, inspirational CDs, and week-long conferences for myself, I was sure that my technicians would get that glimmer of desire in their eye to march right into the next home and come out on top with an upsell. Did this ever happen? Yes, for about two weeks. We had success for a short time; then we went right back into emergency mode. The ship was going under again. Don't get me wrong there were of course feasts, in the midst of the famines but never enough to leave that nice pile of cash at the end of the year. It seemed the magic of owning a business was in the ability of making money vanish.

This was the very reason that we, after a few epiphanies and much research, created The New Flat Rate Menu Pricing System. It's also the reason I have written *Why Won't They Pay Me What I'm Worth*. For years, I went through the same nightmarish cycle in my business, and for years I felt as though I was swimming upstream in hopes that the current would change. The never-ending cycle of disappointment had to stop, and I hope that after you read the following pages, the light will come on and the cycle will stop for you too.

INTRODUCTION

What are you worth as a service provider or businessperson? The truth is, it doesn't matter what you are worth if you can't get your customers to pay it.

The focus of this book is the service industry providers: plumbers, electricians, and HVAC professionals. But these principles can be applied to any onsite service provider—carpet cleaners, painters, pest control companies, and any in-home service company. At some point, if not every single day, these businesses will give away work or valuable skills for almost nothing.

How does it feel to acknowledge that after rigorous and extensive training, and years of experience, you may not be getting paid what you are worth? I'm not saying your current income isn't enough, but when you place a value on your work, the numbers might not add up. The truth is, your pay is probably disproportionate to your worth! Many are making up for it with sheer volume by working longer hours and trying to acquire more customers. Or sadly, the impact is not immediate; they notice it on the backend when they find that they can never retire or quit because there is not enough money to build a suitable retirement.

Getting paid what you are worth should be a top priority, especially when you've dedicated time and effort to your craft. I hope this helps you like it helped me!

Your worth essentially boils down to one factor: Your price. So my next question is a hot one: What is your price? What value are you placing on *you*? Let's face it; your price is your power! When you set it firmly in place and back it up with skills that hold true, you set up your future for the success you envisioned when you started.

Think about it: If you can't get the price you ask for, you can't build your financial strength, and you can't keep up with the market. Nor can you obtain the best tools, equipment, and materials that help you to do the best quality work. *Yes, your price is your power. Without it, you are just another person in a pickup truck.*

While reading this book, I believe you're going to have a few "aha" moments! I bet that by seeing what preventable mistakes I made, some of you will laugh and say, "That's me too!" But by the end, I will share with you how I stumbled upon worldwide industry-changing solutions. You will see that you can get your price and be paid what you are truly worth. It's not impossible! As a matter of fact, it's the exact opposite.

Success does not happen overnight; it takes strategy and ultimately a plan. And we know that all business plans require money. How many times have you tried to put a plan into action with no money? I recently took a phone call from one of my clients who is currently using my automatic selling system. I asked how his company was doing and his reply was, "We have $40,000 in a savings account thanks to you! I'm just calling to ask what I should do with it." That is a nice problem to have. They have no business plan but plenty of money. I think most businesses are just the opposite: They have no money and are working on a business plan.

Cash is where the money is. Cold, hard cash is the power that fuels any business—not assets such as trucks, buildings, or brands. I'd much rather sit down to write a business plan with a bank full of money, wouldn't you?

So what's the problem? The problem is the advice you take. It is usually from people who don't need money because they don't own a business, or they have been successful in business and don't remember what it's like to be broke. Either way, their philosophies of change can be difficult to follow because you might not have the money to do it the way they suggest. *And if you are like me, you have probably gone into debt buying hopes and dreams that were supposed to solve your problems.* If you have done that, stop it right now. Let's put you on the path to making real change with real, tangible impact—impact that will carry you out of the trenches and into the winner's circle.

1

SKILLED CRAFTSMEN —A LIFETIME OF LESSONS

In June of 1970, I heard the dreaded words that changed my life forever: "Get out of bed and get in the truck." Yuck! I was 15 years old and had just finished the 10th grade. Evidently, in my dad's mind, that meant I should get off my lazy you-know-what and help my brothers with electrical wiring for the family business. As the third of five brothers in a family of eight siblings, I had enjoyed every minute of every summer I'd ever lived. Riding my bike all over town, camping in the woods, and swimming in the local pool was all I wanted and expected for my short Minnesota summers.

When I was only 4 years old, my dad, a union electrician working in the iron mines of northeastern Minnesota, saw an opportunity to go west across Minnesota to buy a little electrical company in the small town of Hallock, Mn. Eleven years later, it was my turn to help the family business and earn my spending money for the summer.

Like my brothers and a couple of local men who were darn good electricians, I was expected to pack my lunch and ride the truck wherever the work was needed. On a typical day, we might be installing new motors, controls, and explosion-proof lighting in a grain elevator. Or we could be crawling through an attic digging through a foot or more of fiberglass insulation, looking for the top of a wall over a kitchen, bedroom, or living room to drill a hole and drop a wire down to one of our fellow electricians so we could install a new outlet for a toaster, microwave oven, or some teenage girl's newest can't-live-without necessity, the hot-steam hair curlers.

Believe it or not, a new product like a microwave oven with the warning, "This appliance must be plugged into a dedicated 120-volt 20-ampere circuit," created millions of dollars of electrical work all over the world. Today, you would think nothing of buying a small appliance like a toaster, mixer, or portable icemaker and just plugging it into the nearest receptacle. But back in the day, you might blow out all the lights in the house by doing that.

On my first full day working with my brothers, Gary and Wayne, the three of us crammed into the front of a 1968 Ford van with the words *Hallock Electric* painted on both sides in bold letters. Arriving at one of the many surrounding farm homes, we got out of the van. As I began to walk toward the home where I assumed we would be working, Wayne gave a sharp whistle and a holler for me to get back to the van. Then he grabbed one of my arms while Gary took the other and started kicking me in my rear end while "apprenticing me" on the fact that you never get out of the truck without first putting on your tool belt. They must have been great teachers because now, some 46 years later, I wouldn't think of doing electrical work without a tool belt around my waist. Wayne also instructed me on where to place the outlets, light switches, and light fixtures when wiring a new house, as well as how to read electrical blueprints and where to drill the holes in the new two-by-fours.

Wayne taught me that working fast was profitable for the company. He liked to beat the clock; he wanted us to drill all the holes for wires in a new home before we stopped for morning coffee. Gary and I preferred to drink our coffee while we carefully considered the best places to drill those holes.

Gary was the meticulous one. He taught me that if you did the work very carefully, you would be proud to sign your name to it, which would also be profitable for the company. He would demonstrate exactly how to make up a junction box, bring all the many-colored wires in at least eight inches and route the appropriate wires to each corner, then make a 90-degree bend while bringing the wires out to a clean-cut end. As thorough as he was, Gary also loved saving time. He usually drove 80 mph between service calls just to save the company a few precious minutes.

SKILLED LABOR

What does it mean to be skilled? Per my definition, it is acquired over time and is to work in a trade that requires the ability to use tools or equipment to fix, change, or install things.

Being an electrician in Minnesota and most other states requires an apprenticeship. This means you must work alongside someone skilled so they can train you and it may include some classroom study. The apprenticeship usually lasts two years, at which time you are expected to take your first electrical exam, "The Journeyman Test."

Developing from apprentice to master tradesman takes even more time. I believe it usually takes about 10 years of working at a skilled trade to be exposed to enough obstacles and difficulties to be able to solve them in a moment's time.

Years ago, I knew a guy who was a backhoe operator. Because of the number of years he had operated one, he was truly a skilled craftsman. One day while on the job site, he was operating the machinery, and his father was in the hole they were digging. Out of nowhere, one of the sides of the hole collapsed, burying his father completely. He had only seconds to act. Without hesitation, he scooped out a portion of the dirt on one side to relieve pressure and allow his father to be uncovered. He was inches away from gas lines, electrical lines, and not to mention his father's head. Because of his experience over time and confidence in working in his trade, he not only saved his dad's life, but he did no extra damage to the job site. I'm sure he would have if he had to, but he knew exactly what to do under extreme pressure because he had mastered his skill.

Skilled labor was once passed on through apprenticeship and experience, with older, seasoned craftsmen passing on the secrets of fabricating repairs and services with precision. It was work that good servicemen would be proud to sign their names on. And it paid well.

WHY HAS IT LOST VALUE?

Think about it: A hundred years ago, the average household had one refrigerator, one toilet, and one car. They needed their investments to last. If you view the average household today, you see that the need has not changed, but there is increased access and pressure to replace those investments. People today still want longevity; they just need to be reminded. Skilled laborers were rare. Communities had one skilled laborer in specialty trades such as doctors, mechanics, welders, or electricians. These men and women were highly valuable because they protected the investments of their customers. People were willing to pay and didn't have to be convinced of the value of this kind of work. Not to mention the value was great because those investments were necessary in life, and still are.

The value of skilled labor has only decreased because of the value placed on the things we're skilled at fixing, and the service industry is partially responsible for that devaluation. HVAC technicians would rather replace a unit than fix it and guarantee their company five more years of service calls maintaining that unit. Sure, the replacement revenue is nice, but why not enjoy the long tail of a few more years of repair opportunities and then replace the unit?

Plumbing, HVAC, electrical, carpet cleaning, duct cleaning, pest control, roofing, and many other services are still needed every single day in the lives of homeowners and business owners. The need has not decreased—just the idea of what this labor is worth. Let's start adding it back.

THE LAW OF UNINTENDED CONSEQUENCES

I always stop for red lights, but seldom for blue:
Paul Koop

I laugh every time I think about how the federal government was toying with the speed limits across the country at the time I was graduating from high school in 1973. In 1974, the president signed the 55-mph speed limit into law dropping our country cruising from a pleasurable 65 mph to a yawningly boring 55 mph ride. We were in an energy crisis and needed to decrease our gas consumption, and the thought was that slowing down the rate of traffic on highways might save a few precious barrels of oil somewhere.

This is when the *Law of Unintended Consequences* took effect. People in general don't like being told what to do. Somehow, the new speed limit spurred on some minor rebellion. For example, if I now had to drive 55 mph in areas I knew were patrolled, then I would drive much faster to make up for it where there was no police presence. Thus, the Law of Unintended Consequences was put into effect.

In 1974, radar had not yet been standardized for patrol cars. Instead, the highway patrol officers relied on three other methods to determine your speed. The first method, visual awareness, was where officers were expected to determine your actual speed within 5 mph, using nothing but their own eyes. Can you believe we believed that? If I was driving west down the highway, and an officer met me going east while I was driving 70 mph, he could write me a ticket for anywhere from 65 to 75 mph, and I would simply have to pay the ticket. Fighting a speeding ticket was unheard of! The second method was also a bit shady and still depended on the officer's visual ability. It was a simple calculator called *VASCAR* (Visual Average Speed Computer and Recorder.) If the officers thought you were speeding, they clicked the first switch on the built-in calculator, and it would visually sight your location on the highway. When your car passed the patrol car, the officers would click the second switch. Then when they passed the same location they spotted you at in the first place, they would click the third switch. The mini-computer calculated your average speed, and if it was over 55 mph, you were getting pulled over. The third method was to simply drive up behind you and match your speed. All three methods had the same consequence. You paid the ticket, no questions asked.

With change comes invention and by 1974, the CB Radio was on the rise, becoming the new electronic must-have in your car, directly after the 8-track tape player. Why? Because they wasted no time at all in solving this speed limit crisis.

A typical scenario would play out like this: You were driving on a sparsely populated highway just minding your own business going 55 mph. Suddenly, you would be passed by a car with two large antennas rising off the rear bumper flailing in the wind – because this car was going 90 mph! A minute or two later, another car with large antennas would also speed past you. You realized these two vehicles were communicating. Both directions of the highway had cars with CB antennas watching for cops and giving out locations of highway patrol cars. When they approached an area they knew was being patrolled, they slowed down to 55 mph. Many people eventually realized that it was "safe" to pull behind one of these high-speed vehicles and enjoy life in the fast lane.

The 55-mph speed limit that was intended to reduce speed, save lives, and gasoline, had the unintended effect of provoking traffic to speeds much greater than the 65-mph limit which had previously been in effect. It made the highways more dangerous and increased the consumption of gasoline, which was what we were supposed to be saving in the first place.

I made eight round trips from Minnesota to Los Angeles during that period, and well, let's just say I made good time.

Has any good come from the 55-mph speed limit? Certainly, but the Law of Unintended Consequences proves that effects of decisions, good or bad, are often much farther reaching than originally planned.

So what does this have to do with your business? Let's take a look.

THE DREAM

Why are you a contractor? Did you get bit by the entrepreneurial bug that was so well explained by Michael E. Gerber in his billion-copy-selling book The *E-Myth*? Did you want to be independent? Perhaps you thought you could do a better job than your former boss? Or did you want to keep all the money for yourself instead of making someone else rich? Maybe you wanted to start a family business? There could be hundreds of reasons why you became a contractor. But the real question is, how is that decision working out for you so far?

Let's take this quick survey of what you have acquired so far in your business.

1. Are you happy?
2. Are you wealthy or financially free?
3. Do you have time for your family, friends, and hobbies?
4. Are you as successful as your friends who chose the corporate or more traditional route for their careers?
5. Will you have a nice retirement one day?

If even one of these scenarios is true for you, then that's a good start! But starting and running a business require vision and fortitude. By *vision,* I mean a picture of what you think being in business looks like. Your intention is to see that vision take shape. Your intention is to succeed.

I have a friend who had an excellent job teaching engine repair at a local high school. He and his students were able to work on their personal cars, motorcycles, and off-road vehicles on a regular basis, and they could even use school time to ride and test their work. On top of this great job, my friend had a side business fixing motorcycles at his home. He had a nice three-car garage all set up for motorcycle repair. And he raced motorcycles on the weekends.

He eventually got bitten by the entrepreneurial bug, and the Law of Unintended Consequences kicked in. Oh, and by the way, as terrible as it may sound, this is a true story.

You see, my friend's evenings and weekends were getting overtaken by his hobby of fixing motorcycles. He had a constant backlog of this work, and he never seemed to be able to catch up. Plus, it paid a lot better than the salaried position at the school. One day he made the jump: He decided to go full-time as a motorcycle repairman. He quit his salaried position at the school and hung out a sign for his new motorcycle shop.

In three days, he finished every motorcycle repair job he had and realized he was now out of work and out of a job. Those three-car garage bays that had always been full of work waiting to be done only held about a three-day supply, and then they were empty.

Over the next two weeks, a couple of jobs trickled in, but he soon realized he would have to go back and find a real job. Going back to the school wasn't an option. He would have to find a new one.

The Law of Unintended Consequences took away his salary, his cushy job, and even his retirement account. His intention was to do better than he had been doing by being in business for himself. It wasn't his intention to lose everything. Now he has a much more demanding job and less time in the evenings and weekends to work on his hobby.

Many of us can relate to this story but have the wisdom to not jump off the ledge. Those of you who did, however, might be regretting it, or maybe you just need some redirection and refocus. Nobody can fully control all aspects of their business, especially when they're up against the Law of Unintended Consequences.

THE REALITY

When it comes to hiring exceptional personnel, this law plays a major role. It can happen even when you make all the right moves. You hire clean, sharp, intelligent technicians with selling and communication skills. You invest in them by providing nice uniforms, trucks, tools, and state-of-the-art sales training. Then they quit. Or maybe they stay but fail to reach their full potential.

Let's examine some possible results. You could be experiencing many of these right now.

Expected Results:

- ✓ Your technicians have good attitudes.
- ✓ Your technicians are team players.
- ✓ Your technicians love their jobs.
- ✓ Your technicians always find the opportunities when they are on the job site.
- ✓ Your technicians always present a clear picture of the benefits and advantages of buying more repairs or services the same day.
- ✓ Your technicians always get good responses from the customers.
- ✓ The average service tickets are high.
- ✓ A good percentage of customers buy new equipment.
- ✓ The customers are satisfied and keep coming back, so the business flourishes with cash constantly coming in.

LESS DESIRABLE RESULTS:

- ✗ Your technicians constantly underperform.
- ✗ Your technicians regularly overlook obvious opportunities to upsell.

- ✖ Your technicians keep selling only one task or repair.

- ✖ Your technicians don't seem to care about what is best for the customers.

- ✖ Your technicians don't seem to care about what is best for the company.

- ✖ Your technicians complain and don't show good team spirit.

- ✖ Your technicians quit and go where they think the grass is greener.

- ✖ Your technicians seem to get it and perform but eventually quit for one reason or another.

If your results are mostly positive, then your strategy is fairly effective. If you have been experiencing a few results from each group, then you may need to tweak what you're doing a little bit. However, if you are experiencing multiple less desirable results, it's probably safe to say that what you're doing is not working. You need to make a change.

What happens when you try to fix the problems? Most of the money you spend will have the unintended consequence of not producing what you want, and it will have the undesired effect of continuously raising your overhead. The reason? Every dime you spend on trying to make it work goes straight to the overhead, and ultimately, your business is now more expensive to run.

I struggled with this vicious cycle for years. In order to survive, I had to constantly increase my prices, and the increase in the prices meant more pressure on my technicians to sell and upsell, which indefinitely required more money spent on sales training and tools. I think even my banker was amazed at how fast I could blow money.

Why is the Law of Unintended Consequences so awful? Because it causes your overhead to go higher than you ever wanted it to go. It drives your closest associates and employees away, and all those promises of a profitable business are unveiled to be some of the biggest lies ever told.

So why is it that when you do what seems right, you still get negative results? To find the answer, we must delve deeper into the process that often takes place in service companies. And that is what we will do next.

THE FANTASY FERRIS WHEEL

If you plan to stay in business and grow that business, I have some good and bad news for you. First the bad news: According to a recent statement I heard, in the HVAC industry, over 80% of contractors lose money the first year that their contracting sales exceed one million dollars. The good news, though, is that there is a solution!

I remember thinking I'd finally made it when my annual sales first exceeded a million dollars, that is until my accountant showed me that when I counted the quarter of a million dollars I had to borrow from my bank I had actually lost over $300,000 dollars.

Why is it that what seems so good can carry so much dead weight? I like to compare it to a Ferris wheel. You take a ride on the Ferris wheel expecting an exhilarating experience, going around and around and seeing the whole world from the top. The problem is, however, that it eventually ends, and you're right back where you started, on the ground. And you have less money than when you started. In the business world, I coined it as the *Fantasy Ferris Wheel*. Just like the one at the amusement park, you must pay to ride. But the reason you ride it is that you truly believe at the end of the ride, you will be much better off than when you started.

Here is how the process might have begun for you.

1.   You were once a technician—a good technician—but you were underappreciated and underpaid, so you quit, and you ended up starting your own company. There's your first round on the Fantasy Ferris Wheel. You are going up up and away and it all looks good.

2.   On the second round, you hire technicians. You try to appreciate them more than you were appreciated. You pay them better than you were paid. And they perform—but not quite as well as you performed.

3.   And the third round: You spend more money. You want to improve your technicians' performance, so you get them a nice truck, nice uniforms, and nice tools, and you pay for their training. You show them how much they are appreciated, and you begin a career path for them. You even give them more money. You train them in one or more methods to make it easy for them to be more productive and profitable on the job. It all seems to be working.

4.   Of course, this costs you money. You must pay to ride the Fantasy Ferris Wheel. But the good news is you don't have to pay for it out of your pocket. Instead, you can raise your prices. The easy way to do that is to raise the billable hour in your flat rate books and charge it right back to the customers.

5.   On the fourth round, you spend more money, this time on the company. You join an organization and go to meetings and seminars, and you receive training. You implement new systems

and better training for the techs. You hang out a big carrot by showing them how much money they can make if they do a great job—like other technicians are doing in other companies. You pressure them to perform, but you raise their pay and give better incentives. You give them commissions, piece pay, performance pay, bonuses, spiffs, and incentives.

6. Doesn't this cost you money? Oh yeah, you're into the big bucks now. You are paying out every month, sometimes every week, to grease the bearings on your Ferris wheel, but it's worth it, isn't it? Because when you get this machine finally working right, you'll be able to relax and watch it run like a well-oiled machine. No problem on the money, you just raise your billable hourly rate once again. And so the results are better—for a while.

7. Now onto the *fifth* round. Some of the technicians quit. After all the appreciation you gave them and the money you spent training and paying them, they quit. Unbelievable! And they took all your knowledge, secrets, and training and went to work for your competitor.

8. Now you must start over. You hire better techs and train them. You have learned from your mistakes. You increase the spending, investing more money in marketing and advertising to make up for the customers you lost by your techs going somewhere else and telling your competitor who your big-spending clients were. It all costs a lot of money, but you charge it to the customer by raising that billable hour *again.*

9. Sixth round. Now the prices are getting high, so the technicians' closing rates decrease. Their performance is even worse. You get everybody back on the Ferris wheel and go around again, this time with another version of the same things. You try to get the technicians to sell more and work harder to ensure the financial stability of the company, but they keep underperforming. Do you feel the stress yet?

It's not just recruiting, hiring, and training that is costing you. It's everything you invest in to make it work this time like joining expensive business groups, some costing up to $50,000 or more. You can experiment with sales programs for $10,000 and up. You can even try hiring consultants. The last time I did that it cost me $14,000. You learn from everything, and your employees just want to make a living, your problem it seems, is not their problem.

Now the technicians have poor attitudes and poor morale. They either quit or underperform. The good ones are good, sometimes very good, until they become overpaid, underperforming assets. Or by the time they realize how good they are, they become free agents and go on the open market. As you know, some of them will take all that business knowledge you paid for and use it to start a competing business, trying to take your customers away. After all, they believe that the customers love them, not you.

You try to convince yourself that what you are doing is working, and you think of all the other contractors who say it works for them. But your real problem is that the service technicians just don't do what you know they can do.

Somebody must have the answer. It's time to bring out the big guns. You hire a consultant to work with your people on a weekly and even daily basis to prove to them that it can be done and that by doing it, they can make big bucks and have a great future.

It reminds me of one of my favorite songs when I was a kid, "Snoopy vs. The Red Baron." It went like this: "10, 20, 30, 40, 50, or more, the bloody Red Baron was rolling up the score." But for me, it was $10,000, $20,000, $30,000, $40,000, $50,000, or more that I spent on every new thing that was supposed to make my business model work. For about five years, I felt like I was stuck on this giant Ferris wheel, going around and around.

Then, finally I began to take a hard look around, and I found that I wasn't alone. Other contractors were lining up buying their tickets to join in on the Fantasy Ferris Wheel. The business model was reproducing competitors.

The rides on the Fantasy Ferris Wheel won't get better. They will just get more expensive. The training will never end because no technician or employee can keep up that pace over and over without burning out, getting mad, or quitting. And when they quit, you are left at the bottom of that big steel wheel all alone.

Can you afford to take another ride?

THE POOL JUST GOT SMALLER

The Law of Unintended Consequences has affected all of us at some point, especially if we are in business and especially if you're still reading this book! We have all needed to solve some major problems in our companies. Our first line of defense has always been to get our employees to sell more in order to save our ship from going under. But it seemed like everything we tried was just another round on the Ferris wheel of business. The admission costs were high, but the results were constantly disappointing. However, we were told it could work! We just needed to hire better people. So we went looking for better technicians. But guess what? The pool that once seemed to brim over with good help now barely comes up to our knees. The pool represents the number of technicians who are available for work in our area, specifically, the number of technicians who are willing to do the selling and upselling necessary for success. So why has it gotten smaller?

WHAT'S THE DIFFERENCE?

Most service companies have an ideal technician in mind. Characteristics typically include trade skills, sales skills, dynamic personalities, and solution-oriented capabilities. The industry promotes this binary superhero able to sell an entire system change-out in less than 10 minutes and then install it blindfolded. Who is this guy and why doesn't he work for me? You caught yourself thinking that, didn't you?

A CHANGE IN EXPECTATION

The year 2000 was a banner year across the globe. It was the first year in the history of the world that factory workers were paid better than skilled laborers. Manufacturing was growing, and to get sufficient help, they began to offer the same or better wages than what the local plumbers, electricians, and service companies were offering. They also gave benefits such as health insurance, retirement packages, and 401Ks. Most of the small plumbing and electrical companies had never provided health insurance to their workers. So with the rise in demand for a working force, manufacturing took the workers away from the skilled section.

At that time, we (the skilled labor companies) began to see that most service technicians had no desire or ambition to sell and upsell, so we went looking for those who would and could. We needed clean, sharp, articulate men and women who had technical abilities but also good communication skills. We searched for ambitious, motivated self-starters who would bring in the cash for the promise of a piece of it.

Thus began the introduction of incentives, perks, bonuses, and performance pay. These incentives were typically offered across the board, but the new kind of service tech, the "selling tech," was much easier to motivate than the average serviceman. So the selling techs were patted on the back and paid lucratively while the regular servicemen were underappreciated and made to sit through "rah-rah" sessions while watching all the "star techs" receive high praise.

What happened next surprised everyone. The new selling techs became more than just employees; they became prima donnas. They were capable of bringing lots of money back to the boss so they became entitled, not only to more money but also to better work, better conditions, and better hours. They began to cherry pick the service calls, deciding which they would go on and which they wouldn't. Then another surprise: They became free agents looking for the highest bidder—and so they quit.

The Ferris wheel didn't stop there. The new selling technicians also quit working for that competitor. And because they knew the trade secrets that we had taught them, they started their own companies and became our competitors. The next step was for them to begin hiring away our remaining technicians.

Like I said in Chapter 3, the business model was reproducing competitors. But it was also producing more victims for the disheartening and cruel Fantasy Ferris Wheel.

What came next? They hired one or two of our disgruntled techs, and our personal Ferris wheel ride, the ride that became horrifying, would now begin turning for them.

If this is you, how's that working out for you? I hurt just thinking about it.

REJECTED A SKILL FOR AN IDEA

The pool of available talent got shallower than ever before. Contractors rejected the skilled service technicians who could fix the heck out of about anything, just because they didn't have the knack for sales. Instead, we gave the "star selling techs" all of our attention and ultimately, a sendoff to join or become our competitors.

You see how the pool keeps getting smaller? But wait, there's more. Someone else is looking too.

To make things even more difficult, now, you're not alone on the search for good technicians. There is a swarm of companies coming for your team.

- Utility companies want in on home services.
- Insurance companies want in on home services.
- Uber startups want in on home services.
- Amazon wants to hire plumbers.
- Angie's List wants to hire techs.

Are you getting the point? Anyone in this industry who wants to run service trucks and employ technicians must acknowledge that the game has changed. If you want to survive, then there is an immediate shift that must be made. These new companies taking on the service industry are outfitted with cutting-edge technology, next generation support, and unlimited resources. It will be almost impossible to stop them. You will either have to beat them or join them.

I remember when my biggest concern was that the Sears Company would kill my business with their enormous marketing power. Sears did take a huge piece of the market, but their Goliath ways kept them from putting us all out of business. They had a shot but kept missing the mark.

Utility companies have taken an enormous piece of the in-home service pie in many parts of the country as well, and they have only just begun to get a taste of that easy profit. Fortunately, they also are slow-moving beasts, but the effect has still been devastating to many small companies.

The pool of labor and available customers is shrinking. At this point, you have about three choices.

1. Quit the business and get out while you can, maybe even sell out to a large company and come out okay.
2. Keep doing the same thing you've always done and stay on the Ferris wheel.
3. Keep reading!

TECH VERSUS SALESMAN

After about 10 years on the Fantasy Ferris Wheel, I acknowledged that if I were spending hundreds of thousands of dollars on my business model, and it had no real lasting results, then maybe I had the wrong model, or perhaps there was a flaw in it. So I took a hard look.

I mean when a skilled trades headhunter says that most companies are now hiring four techs hoping for just one who will stay, heck, even getting four qualified applicants in the door is a daunting challenge these days! This alone should make you question your approach.

When I stumbled upon the answer, I must admit it changed my entire outlook on the service business. I couldn't believe I hadn't seen it years earlier because it was glaringly obvious. The reason I had been blind to it is that I am not a true service tech; I am an entrepreneur. I've always been upwardly mobile, looking for better ways to succeed in the service industry. My business model was essentially that service technicians must sell and upsell when in front of my customers. But I was trying to hire skilled craftsmen who *never wanted to sell in the first place*.

It's true that our trade school classrooms continue to remain on low volume. Our average technician earns over $40,000 a year with only minimal education debt, so why do we still need so many workers? Employee retention is low and doesn't seem to be increasing. Our problem: A low-volume pool of technicians. But maybe the problem is not the number of workers we need to hire to stay profitable; maybe the problem is that we're hiring the wrong guy.

TWO ENTIRELY DIFFERENT POOLS—THE TECHNICIAN AND THE SALESMAN

If we analyzed the core values and drive of a true service technician, the industry would see some compelling features. Most service technicians are hands-on junkies. It's the thrill of the fix. These men and women possess an innate desire to serve and find solutions. Their reward doesn't come from the bottom line; it comes from fixing the problem. It comes from leaving a home in better working order than when their work boots first hit the floor. Trueborn technicians aren't salesy or cunning; they are get-to-the-point, fix-the-problem, ease-your-pain kinds of people. Their goal: The hum of a solved problem. Rarely do you find servicemen who are fully dedicated to fixing things who also enjoy going into the home, putting on their portable suit and tie to make a sale, and then changing in the service truck to fix the unit. These men and women get their reward by being recognized as hard workers with a skillset to fix the problem and leave the home secure. They have no real desire to upsell or make a profit. Their profit is a happy homeowner—not a happy business owner.

What differentiates the service techs from the salesmen? Well, the bottom line, to start. The salesmen's sense of accomplishment doesn't stem from turning the heat back on; it stems from the win, the final sale, the signature on the bottom line. Clarifying and convincing the customers of their need for certain machinery is something technicians aren't inherently interested in. Making more, selling more, adding more, and negotiating is the lifeblood of interaction for salesmen. Their goal is to change the outcome of the initial service call. Can they have technical skill? Yes. Can they be great at fixing things? Yes. But is that what drives them? No, not at all.

OUR INABILITY TO DISTINGUISH

What happens to the technicians when contractors don't know who to hire? Well, it looks a little like this:

1. Contractors expect their servicemen to put on their truck driver hat and drive to the customer's home or business,

2. then put on their communicator hat and greet and build a rapport with the customer.

3. Next, they must put on their skilled technician hat and diagnose the problem.

4. Once they find today's problem, they must put on their detective hat and look for more problems/opportunities and make a list of everything that the customer could buy from them today.

5. Now, they need a statistician's hat to look up the prices of each item before they put on their mathematician's hat.

6. Why? Because now it's time to do some math and apply discounts in case the customer buys more.

7. Once the techs have the numbers right, they must put on their creative genius hat and put it all together in a perfect presentation so they can put on their salesman hat and show the customer what they have found and what they are recommending that they buy.

8. The customer will have objections, but the technicians must use the sales training we bought for them and overcome those objections.

9. The customer might not want everything on the list, so the technicians can put on their statistician, creative genius, and mathematician hats and repackage the task. Then they must do the math again, present it again, overcome more objections, and finally get to a point where the customer is willing to agree to buy.

10. Then they must neatly write or create an invoice and get the signature.

11. Then they will put on their service tech hat and do a high-quality job and actually fix the problem.

12. Then they must put on their sales hat again and collect the money. In the end, they'll jump back in the truck and head to the next job.

13. The kicker: At the end of the day, they have to hand all that hard-earned cash over to you.

Then they must do it all over again, and again, and again! Who came up with this idea? How did we ever get sold this bill of goods?

THE FIRST SOLUTION

First you must acknowledge that personality and desired skillset play a huge factor in whether someone would naturally fit into your available position. It's mere psychology. To some of us, selling is a natural skill.

To others, it's not. There is no way you're getting them to sell. How do we fix this? It's simple. Let someone else sell for the technicians or provide a system that allows the customer to buy without requiring the technicians to sell. The faster you accept that techs are techs and salesmen are salesmen, the faster your budget will expand and the better chance you have of a stable growing business.

Keep reading. There is more to the answer.

RETAIN YOUR SKILLED LABOR

True servicemen don't want to keep moving around from company to company. These men and women have no desire to start their own company. They only quit when they feel they are forced to. They, like you, want to be respected and appreciated for their acquired skill, and they want to be paid what they are worth.

Fifty years ago, we could do the work, send the bill, and get paid. No questions asked and no awkward moments for our innocent technicians having to collect our money. Why? Because there was no focus on parts. People never questioned the cost. There was little ability, or even desire, to research the cost of the job—and Amazon wasn't selling capacitors for $5 for the do-it-yourselfers to install themselves.

Now that our rates have continued to increase, immediate sales resistance has increased with it. In addition, we want our technicians to upsell in an already uncomfortable situation. This newfound resistance makes it difficult to keep any morale with our technicians. One of their core values is to find solutions and relieve the customer's pain. The constant increasing of rates makes them feel and appear to be the bad guys.

It's an easy task to keep technicians happy. These men and women only require the compliment of good work and a little pat on the back from time to time. However, what most technicians hear in today's world is, "Why didn't you charge to program that? Didn't you notice that the toilet wasn't working? A customer called and said you didn't even tell them this. Why didn't you check that? Why didn't you do this?" All the technicians are hearing is that they are coming up short and that you don't appreciate the craftsmanship and skill they bring to the table. Instead, they are pressured to sell, sell, and sell. This is not what they signed up to do. They didn't take this job to make you rich; they signed up to fix things.

Is This How Others Do It?

Much of the frustration in business comes from the fact that we keep pushing the Law of Unintended Consequences. Are other industries doing the same thing? Let's compare a few.

A major life insurance company will take 1,000 applications for one of their sales job postings. They will then look for individuals who can sell life insurance and want to make a career out of it. Out of 1,000 applicants, only three will get the job because only three had the skills needed to succeed. The other 997 will not make the cut, even though they actually wanted a job in sales.

How many electricians, plumbers, heating and air technicians, etc., signed up for a sales job? Most contractors I speak with say that only 10–20% of typical service technicians can or will sell, and if they will, it's a chore.

Have you ever noticed that in the automotive industry, if you need an air conditioner installed in your vehicle, your automotive mechanics will almost never talk to you? They certainly don't sell you any work. If you go to a Ford, Chevy, or Chrysler dealer, you'll talk to service writers or managers, rarely the mechanic. The men or women out front will communicate with you, contract with you for the work, and sell and upsell if any upselling is available. Then they simply tell the mechanics what you bought. The technicians in the automotive industry do not have a selling position. Nor were they even expected to.

Next, let's take a look at IBM Computers. IBM began as a hardware company. Actual salesmen were hired to sell IBM products to businesses. Around 1975, you could buy an IBM computer, but without IBM's installers, it wouldn't do a thing. IBM had to bring in computer installers to set up the equipment and computer programmers to write the software and make it work. Those two particular positions didn't sell anything. They were in the technical department, and that was their only task. IBM would never adopt a business model where their technical employees did the selling. IBM used professional salesmen to sell their products, technicians to install the equipment, and programmers to program.

Plumbing, electrical, and HVAC companies might be all alone in saying, "This is my business model: I want my technicians to be able to sell and upsell in the home and bring the money back to me."

THE SELLING TECHNICIAN

THEY DO EXIST

There are men and women who are both technically competent and sales-savvy out there in the world. They do exist! In addition to being able to make repairs, they have communication and sales skills. They can sell and upsell. They can overcome objections. They can close the sale. They can negotiate a better deal. They can repackage the product and bring the customer back to the table, over and over. But we all know that this is a rare combination because these people are not service persons, they are in fact entrepreneurs. Entrepreneurs are on a career path, and the end of that path is a business of their own. It's as simple as that.

6

THE CLONING MYTH

There is a reason Frankenstein was called a monster.

Rodney Koop

THE CLONE MACHINE

Do you really want your employees to be carbon copies of you? Is cloning the answer?

In August of 2007, I began to realize that growing a contracting business with the business model I had been instructed to use was quite hopeless. However, I knew that the model had been fashioned by contractors who were considered to be successful and that they were incorporating contemporary methods of business that were considered to be sheer brilliance. It's the thought that running a company is easy and that anyone with the desire to work for themselves can do just that and that they can do it successfully. If you want to be an entrepreneur, you certainly can. There have been millions of dollars made off of those ideas. Rarely do these methods take into consideration the role of unintended consequences and the unfortunate fact that business is not supposed to be a carnival ride and that it is most definitely not for everyone.

Let me show you what I discovered to be the most common and the most troublesome breakdown in trying to build and run a contracting service business.

The main tenets of most businesses would be getting and keeping customers, making a profit on transactions with those customers, and handling the back end of the business such as accounting, payroll, etc.

When it comes to customer acquisition, accounting, payroll, taxes, purchasing and inventory management, customer service, call taking, dispatching, billing, data collection, and customer records management, the work can easily be done in-house, or it can be outsourced.

Finding people who can do the actual technical work itself—diagnosing, troubleshooting, repairing, and maintaining customer's equipment—is not difficult either. Surely you can recruit and hire suitable technicians who can fix and repair your customer's equipment.

The silver tuna that everything rides on is selling the work once a diagnosis is made. If someone doesn't sell the work that the techs recommend, then the techs can't do the work. And if they can't do the work, you can't collect the money and earn the profit you need to be in business. It's as simple as that.

THE GREAT BREAKDOWN

It is the art of selling the work where the breakdown begins. It took years and hundreds of thousands of dollars for me to open my eyes and see it. One day it hit me, and I've never been the same since.

I once was a big proponent of the large-scale business model—the model that convinced the contractors that the solution to their biggest problems would be found in their ability to clone themselves. Do each job yourself, write processes and procedures, and then hire someone to follow suit.

Are You Trying to Clone Yourself?

It's true that when starting a new company, you must get the systems up and running to generate enough business before you can hire additional help. It's true that creating the systems necessary for your future employees while actually doing the work is efficient and thorough. So what is the detrimental factor that almost cost me my business more than once? The thought that if you clone yourself, you can have someone as competent and passionate about your company as you are. But if you clone you, then you have just created someone who will do what you did—leave your employer and start your own business. For 13 years, this is what I did. Needless to say, I have created several competitors.

What has caused this misunderstanding? Let's look at some factors that ultimately did not get me to the winner's circle, just another round on the Fantasy Ferris Wheel. Michael E. Gerber, in his best-selling book *The E-Myth Contractor,* says it like this:

1. Acknowledge to yourself when you are filling employee shoes and when you are filling owner shoes.

2. As an employee, determine the most effective way to do the job you are doing, then document that job. Write it out as this becomes your new process manual.

3. Once you've documented the job, create a strategy for replacing yourself with someone else, who, after learning how to faithfully use the system you've provided, will then teach it to yet another person. [In other words, have your new service technician do exactly what you do as a service technician. Then have the next generation of employees ride with that person so they can learn to do exactly what he or she does, which, supposedly, is to copy what you do as a service technician.]

4. Manage the newly delegated system using your new employees. Improve the system by quantifying its effectiveness over time.

5. Repeat the above process throughout your business wherever you are acting as an employee rather than owner.

6. Leave behind dedicated people using your effective systems, each time moving you out of employee-ship work and freeing you to do ownership work.[1]

This makes perfect sense. If you are doing the job to the best of your ability and satisfaction, then you would want to document it so that someone you hire can be taught the guidelines to replicate the job and get the same result as you. But in the service industry, these "entrepreneur technicians" who would go out to service the customers they acquired, would also have to sell the work once they got on the job, do the work, and then collect the money. This should not be too difficult, right? The contractors knew what they needed to charge and what they thought

---

[1] Gerber, M. E. (2007). *The E-Myth Contractor: Why Most Contractors' Businesses Don't Work and What to Do About It* (pp. 23). Pymble, NSW: HarperCollins e-books.

their work was worth. Therefore, they needed to provide a system for the new technicians to value the work and set a price for it. Again, our industry has pricing books that made that quite easy. And for years, it worked pretty well.

A CHANGE COMES

Two major changes deteriorated the effectiveness of this method. The first was the ever-increasing cost of doing business, paired with the higher prices of the work. Up to about 1997, top-level technicians only needed limited sales ability because there was very little resistance to the price of work. Technicians would simply show up at the job, perhaps diagnose the problem (if the boss hadn't already done it), and then do the repair. The office sold the job, overcame any objections, scheduled the work, and did the pricing, invoicing, and collecting.

HOW SALES TRAINING WAS INTRODUCED TO THE SKILLED TRADE INDUSTRY

If you begin to look at the beginning of sales training, you will see that it wasn't heavily marketed to contractors by way of books, tapes, articles, and seminars until the mid-90s. As the resistance to the price grew, we attempted, with varying rates of success, to train the technicians to become more sales savvy by overcoming the price objection, showing the value of the work offered, and closing the sale. This investment in sales training began driving up costs quickly. Therefore, we were taught to raise our prices to cover these additional costs. The money had to come from somewhere, and that somewhere was the customer. So we raised the billable hour.

THE INFORMATION AGE

The second change was new access to information, which the customers began to use before and after the service call. Customers are undoubtedly more informed today than ever before. However, the quality of that information is questionable. For example, the products and services we provide have been reduced to the level of a commodity, like the price of pork. Now, the technicians are often met not only with price resistance, but also with a customer who knows where to buy the product or service for much less than what you are offering.

You could easily say that I am simplifying the situation by only mentioning two contributing factors. But to get to the solution, we only need the two with the greatest impact to recognize that our current business model is in a continual cycle of failed companies and bankrupted contractors.

In response to the customers' pricing and payment resistance on the upfront, the industry switched out the simple sales systems they had used for quite some time for a system that allowed for no surprises. Why? To eliminate dishonest customers who would not pay or insisted on a reduction of costs. The new pricing model could be an estimate of cost based on labor and materials, or it could be a flat rate cost given out of a pricing guide or flat rate book. Thus, the phenomenon of *Flat Rate Pricing* was introduced.

I say *phenomenon* because this had a huge effect on all types of services, from plumbing to carpet cleaning to maid services. For the first time in history, we, the contractors, gave pricing materials to the technicians. Not knowing how to price services and parts was the primary thing that kept technicians from starting their own companies. Once a company gave them the tools to price jobs, they could price their work for the company or themselves as future owners of new companies.

However, flat rate pricing was not the only or most powerful push to send our former loyal employees scurrying to become our competitors. Sooner or later, there would come a very powerful force pushing them out of our door: Sales training.

THE EXODUS

When I took a close look at why some of my employees left and either went to my competitors or started businesses of their own, I found a trend. The trend was that they would work for one or two more HVAC companies and then eventually start their own businesses—usually within two years of leaving my company. What became of those who did not end up as business owners? Those who wanted to be in the skilled trades and had no desire to do anything else ended up working for very traditional heating, cooling, electrical, or plumbing companies. They could take on a maintenance job in a large plant or perhaps work for a new construction company or a service company that would send out bills to the customer after the work was done. Another outcome: They simply went to a manufacturing plant and got out of the in-home services work altogether, which didn't and still doesn't make our constant search of the talent pool problem any easier.

Thinking entrepreneurs could clone themselves into service technicians was absurd. It sounded good at the time, but it messed up thousands of service techs and financially devastated otherwise sound businesses.

THE HABITUAL BUYER

People buy in 15-second spurts.

—Matt Koop

I'm a sucker for catchy marketing. Really, if an item interests me, I'll hand over some cash. I have a shop full of things I've bought over the years. You might call me a habitual "keeper of things" too. I don't get rid of anything. About ten years ago, I began to study the subject of buying. As a frequent consumer, I was a willing and suitable subject for my studies. I started paying attention to my purchases and took notes to discuss with friends. Then, in turn, I began to observe the buying patterns of the people around me. My findings changed my life and will change yours too.

This interest in habitual buying patterns began when my son, Matt, made a random comment one day saying, "People buy in 15-second spurts." I found that almost too crazy to believe, so I asked him to elaborate. He said, "I was at Best Buy and wanted to buy an iPad. However, there were many people in front of me looking at the same device, and I had to wait my turn. I began to notice that individuals would walk up, swipe the screen a few times and if a salesman were present, they would ask them about the color and size of memory. Then they would either buy or not in 15 seconds."

This didn't seem right; it sounded way too fast. So the next time I was in the grocery store with my wife, I was "aware," watching the other shoppers. My wife looked at me and said, "I need a couple of heads of cabbage." She turned her cart toward the produce section and bee-lined for the cabbages. As she walked, she saw the price and said, "Hmmm, $2 a head. That's not too bad." As she got closer, she eyed two of the eight cabbages in the bin and reached out to touch them. She then touched one or two more and picked up the two she had chosen in her mind and placed them in the cart. Then she immediately pushed her cart down the produce aisle, looking for other items on her list. I timed the event. From the time her cart stopped by the cabbage until she started moving again was less than—you guessed it—15 seconds. Amazing! I thought. I watched her go from item to item, and almost never did she go over the golden time of 15 seconds. Most items were well under that amount.

Thus began my obsession. I started timing people in stores. A big-ticket item like an iPad, laptop, or table saw would often be looked at more than one time before purchasing, but on the day and time of the purchase, it would often go very quickly.

I was in one of my favorite stores, Lowes, and needed to buy a powered miter saw. When I say I needed to buy it, I mean I had looked at the saws several times over the last few months, but today, I needed to cut up some lumber to make raised bed garden boxes for my wife. Everyone knows that when you take on a special project for your wife, you are automatically authorized to buy some power tools. So off to Lowes I went, and again I found myself in the power miter aisle. I looked at the $389 DEWALT, and like Goldilocks, I quickly thought, "Too much." Next, I turned to the $189 Ryobi, and this time I heard Goldilocks say, "Too little." Then I looked at the $260 Rigid miter saw and thought, "Just right." I asked the store employee standing close by, "Is this a good power saw?"

His response was immediate. "No one ever brings that one back."

In my cart it went. The total time in front of the Rigid tool on the day I bought it: about 28 seconds.

I thought, "If I buy fast, I wonder who else buys fast."

So I took this to my business. Service repair calls were the perfect testing ground. If a purchase of a $300 power tool took a few visits to the store and a little time researching, what happens on a service call when something is broken? The scenario is quite different than your typical consumer situation. For example, if my air conditioning quits, and I am taking the morning off work to wait for the technician, what typically happens?

As the customer, I expect the following:

1. A technician will come to my home and accurately determine what the problem is.

2. The technician will be able to fix it and make it run.

3. The company will be reputable enough to stand behind the work.

4. It will cost a little more than I am comfortable paying.

5. The repair will get done, and I will pay for it and get back to work.

What are my fears?

1.   They won't come when they say they will.

2.   They won't be able to fix it today for whatever reason.

3.   They will tell me I need something new for $10,000.

What is my stress level? Pretty darn high.

Do you see that there is a considerable difference between the mental state of a service customer and someone buying a power tool?

However, the expectations before the service call are very similar to the expectations my wife has when she goes to the store to buy cabbages. This is what she expects:

1.   The store will have cabbages.

2.   The store will have good quality cabbages.

3.   She will be able to buy two cabbages today.

4.   The cabbages will cost a little more than when she saw them on sale the last time she was at the store.

Finally, my eyes opened, and I could see the obvious. Although I had witnessed my business achieve great success and horrible failure over and over again, I was fighting against a false premise, an untruth, if you will, that service technicians could and would go into the homes and business to sell and upsell. Finally, one day, I saw the truth—that this was just a fantasy that was keeping me on the up-and-down Ferris wheel. I had to walk away from that premise.

Still dizzy from the spin of the out-of-control Ferris wheel, I got lucky and caught a glimpse of what would change the game entirely. The customers had a habit, a natural tendency to buy; in fact, they love to buy. I realized that if I could harness the habitual buying pattern of the customers, the natural desire to buy my services, then I could stop trying to sell. The game is won when I get out of the way and let them do what they want. Let them flash that credit card and buy more than I could ever sell them even on my best day. That day, the game changed, and I took my first giant step off that Fantasy Ferris Wheel.

We decided to take our study to another level and began looking at menu-style shopping or, to put it simply, ordering at fast-food restaurants. I began going to McDonald's. I would buy a Coca-Cola and take a seat near the counter so I could watch the hungry customers. The typical customer would walk in while looking up at the menu board simultaneously. How people didn't trip and fall, I'll never know. These people fully expected to make a purchase that day. The typical purchase took less than – you got it – 15 seconds.

Sometime in the middle of 2014, I gave this a name: "The Habitual Buying Pattern." I thought that I'd stumbled upon a brilliant discovery and that the world's leading scientists and psychologists would be clamoring to learn about it. Google proved me wrong. I hadn't discovered anything new. The habitual buying patterns of people had been studied by great minds for many years. No surprises there; we are, after all, in a retail-driven society.

However, most research on the matter suggested that consumers operate habitually on cheap trinkets and lower-priced products. It took some time to find research on high-ticket items like vehicles. Eventually, I found that other than it taking more time to decide on cars and other big-ticket items, it still came down to habitual patterns. They either normally bought the cheapest, the middle, or the best. This pertained to the service industry also. When I took my observation into the field, I could see almost identical buying patterns on a $200 service repair, a $2,000 water heater, and a $15,000 HVAC system. Even a whole house generator for $35,000 could have a decision time of less than 30 seconds. How could this be?

The difference I discovered between the in-home purchase as opposed to, say, the purchase of a television, was all in the attitude of the consumers. When our customers arrange their schedules for us to come to their homes, they fully expect to buy something the same day to get it done and over with.

What did I do with this information? I mean, come on; the keys to the kingdom had just fallen in my lap. I realized that technicians hate being our salesmen, and the customers' habitual buying patterns show that no matter what the situation, when sales resistance is removed and choices are present, people will buy almost every single time. So the ultimate question: How are you, the contractor/technician going to position your customers to be in the right frame of mind to say *yes* to your best? I guess you had better keep reading.

8

SHOPPERS, DISCOUNTS, AND OPTIONS

Anytime they give away "free" hot dogs,
it's time to watch your purse!

—David Koop

Still more to learn? Oh yes, but we are nearing the end and heading straight for our solution.

During this time of gathering information and testing my theory of habitual buying patterns, I studied three successful companies: Ford Motor Company, McDonald's Corporation, and The Home Depot. These companies provide services every day to the same clientele that you and I do. Like them or not, they all maintain a large satisfied customer base and return millions of dollars to their owners, and still they can keep a vast workforce of talented people, which allows them to turn out consistently high-quality products. To be concise, we will focus on my experience with one, The Home Depot.

One day, as I was beginning my study of The Home Depot, I asked my daughter Melody to take a ride with me to check something out. She agreed, and we hopped into my car and drove over to the store. Two things were piquing my curiosity. The first question I had was, "Do people follow any pattern when they buy products at The Home Depot?" And secondly, "Do The Home Depot employees use any selling methods or make any attempt to influence customers to buy more than what they had intended to buy when they came to the store?"

SHOPPERS—WHICH ONE ARE YOU?

Our initial intention in The Home Depot that day was to observe people shopping. We were both equipped with watches, and we planned to time how long it took normal, everyday people to make a purchasing decision, no matter the type of purchase. We wanted to see how many people we could find who would make a purchase in 15 seconds or less. The result of that first day evolved into hundreds of trips to retail stores to observe shoppers.

In the evaluation of myself, I noticed that I shop at one or more big-box, Home Depot-like stores almost once per week, somewhere between 35 and 45 visits per year. If they don't like me by now, they should. I was able to begin a study of my personal shopping habits simply because I was there so often, but I found exceptional value in being able to observe my feelings, emotions, and thoughts during my visits.

As a bonus, while watching other shoppers, I observed that there are primarily two kinds of customers at these big-box stores. I also noticed how much they are like the customers who call us to their homes to repair something.

THE "SHOPPER" CONSUMER

The first type of customer I call the "Shopper." These people research and gather data as they go through the store. Their pattern is to go down a row of refrigerators, starting at the most expensive, which is a large, double-door, stainless steel behemoth costing well over $3,000. Most won't go any farther than their interests. Most activity seems to be in the $1,600 to $2,200 area.

The Shopper will almost never buy on the first visit. The first visit is just to gather intel. As a matter of fact, when the store associates ask if they can help them, and the shoppers say, "I'm just looking," they really are just looking. They will look once at The Home Depot and usually once at another similar store.

They then will return with the decision they have made and go straight to the chosen appliance, thus beginning the purchasing process. Typically, they are asking questions on finance, delivery, disposal of their existing fridge, and when the new one can be brought to their house. But in essence, this decision is made before they enter the store for the second time. This time, they came to buy.

The Shopper pattern is repeated with much more detail in kitchen cabinets and with less detail in washers and dryers. Carpeting and flooring get a good bit of this also. There are certain purchases that seem to warrant the significant other having a crucial say in the choice. Lesser items like kitchen faucets and water heaters are often bought in two minutes or less.

Let's evaluate the Shopper's process. While considering The Home Depot shoppers, think about your customers. Where are they in their decision-making process?

1. They are moving toward but are not yet at the purchase moment.
2. They likely have a date in mind, and it is very soon, but the nature of both significant parties agreeing causes a little more time in

the process of buying the bigger-ticket items. You could say they balance emotion with some common sense for these items.

3. Time is not of the essence to them. The world won't end if they don't get it today.

THE "CONTRACTOR" CONSUMER

The second type of customer I observed is what I would call the "Contractor" or the "Do-It-Yourselfer." After all, these are do-it-yourself stores, and the fit is impressive. These customers have an imminent need, and time is of the essence. They are ready to buy now!

There are usually only two things that will cause these customers to leave without buying the entire list. One is the inventory; what they want must be there. The other is the price; the value must be such that they feel comfortable with it. It must be close enough to what they think it is worth that they don't feel the need to drive to another store to compare. If those two things are in order, they will buy it immediately.

If they know full well that they can return whatever they don't use, then they often purchase a few more items than they need or came for. Note: Most of those extra items will not be used or returned.

COMPARISON

If we were to pause and make a simple comparison between these two types of customers, which type would you prefer if you owned the store? The Shoppers are comparing information they have found online and in newspapers, mailers, and marketing pieces in their mind. They are also looking at other stores. Eventually, they will buy, and they will buy larger-ticket items, so there is great value in that. The second type of customers, the Contractors, will almost certainly make one or more purchases before leaving the store. Both types are important, and it is pertinent to note that The Home Depot has a business model that works well for both of them. If I had to choose one or the other, though, I would choose the imminent buyer, the right-now buyer, every time because my competition has almost no chance of taking this buyer away from me. But of course, I want both buyers if I can get them.

Now, take a minute to think about your business and your typical customers.

- Which pattern do they fit?
- Which pattern does your company cater to?
- What's the percentage of each type that buys products and services from you?

DO HABITUAL BUYERS EVEN NEED DISCOUNTS?

It was only a few weeks later while shopping at The Home Depot that I realized big-box stores don't try to save you money by putting more than one item together and giving you a discount. They simply lay it all out, and they allow you to put together what you want for each job. You pay full price for whatever you buy from Aisle 3 and full price for whatever you buy from Aisle 4. That's the retail way. It is very simple, and the customers understand it.

After testing this pricing method, I understood the genius of the big-box store. You simply make a choice from an array of products in the aisle. For example, there will often be as many as 70 kitchen faucets in a big-box store, and you choose without expecting a discount at the cash register. You are happy with your decision on Aisle 3 and also on Aisle 4. You actually "set" or "choose" your own price when you select an item. You feel like you saved money, so there is no need to ask for a discount when you get to the cashier.

OPTIONS PROMOTE FAST DECISIONS

By this time, while timing buyers, we noticed another pattern. This may sound funny, but you can observe it yourself at any store or fast food restaurant. What we noticed was that people would find the section of the store that had what they wanted and stop in front of the particular object they wanted to buy. We watched as they moved their heads up, then down, then left then right, and then reached for the object and put it in the cart—usually in less than 20 seconds.

We also noticed that there were always low-priced objects that seemed to give the customers peace of mind that they had the option to buy something that was easy on the pocketbook. But about eight out of 10 customers would not buy the lowest priced item. This was interesting.

In addition, we saw that when a major retailer had a low-priced option and a high-priced option, there would always be options in between that moved up in a formulated way. They didn't have one item at $1 and one at $15. They had perhaps seven items, and they were priced $1, $2.95, $3.55, $6.85, $9.67, $12.99, and $15.99. We observed that the customers' eyes would move up the list of products, then back down, and then back up to the one they would eventually choose. Again, this was done very fast.

So now I knew how the customers operated. But how could I turn this into the foundation of a successful business model?

ANOTHER HOME DEPOT GOLDEN TICKET

On another day, my daughter Melody and I took off to The Home Depot to do some more testing. When we arrived, I was surprised to find out that a local HVAC company was in the parking lot outside of the main entrance with a couple of tables and a gas grill. They were giving out free hot dogs with the intention of introducing themselves and their HVAC company and perhaps offering some free or reduced rate service.

What happened next caught me off guard. You see; Melody and I parked quite a distance from the entrance because she is young and likes to get exercise in parking lots. Me, not so much. However, as I waited for

her to get out of the car, I noticed a couple exit their car and begin walking toward the main entrance. Then for some reason, they turned abruptly and walked much further to another entrance by the garden supplies. This aroused the Sherlock Holmes in me, and my inner detective sprang into action. I told Melody to hold up and explained to her what I thought I had seen. Then we waited, and sure enough, in only a few minutes, it happened again. Someone got out of their car, started toward the main entrance, and then made an abrupt shift to another entrance.

I began to wonder if it had anything to do with the hot dogs. Maybe they knew something I didn't? I love a free hot dog! Especially when my competitors are paying for them. I watched until I observed a pattern. Three out of 10 people would walk farther to avoid the hot dog stand. If 30% of the population refused to walk by a hot dog stand, there had to be more to it.

I won't say I solved the mystery the first time I saw it. But eventually, I came to realize that a certain percentage of the population is entirely turned off by salesmen. So opposed, in fact, that they will walk further distances to their destinations just to avoid them. Then the mystery was solved, and out of it came what I have come to call "Indisputable Rule No. 1 of Sales." That rule goes like this:

Everybody hates it if you try to sell them something!

The American public recognizes the moniker that, "There is no such thing as a free lunch." The underlying perception is this: "They are giving away hot dogs to somehow ensnare me or attempt to sell me something." This is good stuff.

NO INTRUSIVE SALESMEN

The one thing that was glaringly missing from The Home Depot, Lowes, and other stores were salesmen. No one at The Home Depot ever tried to sell me anything (with the possible exception of the hot dog guys, but they were not employees of The Home Depot). I began to notice that I feel comfortable and secure in this type of environment, and I feel threatened and uncomfortable in a place where a salesman comes up to me and attempts to sell me something.

Just consider what timeshare companies must give away to get you to sit with one of their salesmen for 90 minutes. I have been offered a two-man raft, five days of all-expense-paid vacationing, a cruise to the Bahamas, seven days all paid at a luxury resort, and on and on. That is what it takes to get someone like you and me to listen to a salesman for 90 minutes. Many of you reading this book would not spend 90 minutes with a salesman for all the tea in China.

So why would we think homeowners want us to try to sell them things when what they called us for was to fix something?

THE SOLUTION

Make Something Happen!

– Danielle Putnam

Irealized everything we had done up until this point was based on a business model that was centered around technicians selling and upselling in the home. The two broad and seemingly bulletproof truths to rise out of that model were these: Your techs hate selling, and everyone hates when you try and sell them something.

After all my years as a contractor, paired with the hours upon hours of research, I found we had to solve five major problems that I gratefully ran smack into.

1. Businesses need more money to be profitable, treat employees fairly, and build a legacy for their families and future generations.

2. News media, eBay, Amazon, and former encounters with contractors have trained homeowners to believe that parts are cheap and in-home providers are constantly trying to sell overpriced and unneeded repairs.

3. Service technicians do not want to face the wrath and rejection of homeowners, so they will not follow through with selling and upselling in the home.

4. The expense of trying to train technicians to sell raises overhead so much that most businesses eventually fail.

5. Everybody hates it when you try to sell them something.

THE MENU

We had to completely reevaluate why we were in business and how we could somehow reconcile these major problems. How did we do it? How did we come to the grand solution? The answer: The Menu. I'm not talking about packaging, not bundling, not discounting; just plain and simple menu pricing—like at your favorite fast food restaurant.

A great discovery came out of all our testing. We had to stop what we were doing and make a significant change. So we gave it our all, and

I eventually sold my contracting business and joined full force with my son, Matt, and daughter, Danielle and another daughter Melody. We created *The New Flat Rate Menu Pricing System*. How could we ignore these blatant, in-your-face facts! We were holding years of wisdom and years of plain common sense in our bare hands. We white knuckled our idea, tested it over a five-year period, and perfected it. Our menu is now used over 25,000 times weekly and has turned on the relief valve for contractors all around the globe.

The Secret Sauce: This is where I tell you how to do it. Yes my system will do it for you but if you want to experiment follow this process.

So what exactly is a menu? A menu is when you add value to a product without changing it. To make it easier to grasp, I'll transform it into what we know about menus. Let's look at a modern burger menu.

Burger Upgrades

- Burger
- Cheeseburger
- Double Cheeseburger
- Bacon Cheeseburger
- Half-Pound Burger
- Angus Burger

The point is if you can enhance the value of an item, you can sell it for more. It's the simplest, most powerful selling method devised so far, and it has the added benefit of being the most profitable way to be in business. By simply adding cheese, you get more for the burger and still have the fries to sell as an add-on. Do you see the power? Don't just try to sell the consumers another item. *First, try to get more for what they called you for in the first place.*

Let's delve a little deeper into that last statement because it is the greatest piece of information ever handed out to anyone in business.

Why is it so important to increase the value of the burger before you sell the fries? Because the burger is what the customers want to buy, and if you give them a chance to buy a better burger next to the basic burger, it makes the better burger ten times more appealing. It costs you much less to enhance the value of the basic burger than it does to make an entire batch of fries. Profit must first be maximized on the main event before you offer a second.

Once the customers choose the better burger (and have already committed more money than they would have originally), they add the fries, thus giving you up to eight times more profit than if you had just sold a burger and an order of fries. This is the genius of the fast food business. This model has made the Ray Kroc Family one of the richest families in the world and one of the largest holders of high-priced real estate worldwide.

When we began formulating our menu, first and foremost, we had to standardize it. It was a must that we make it easy to learn, easy to use, and most importantly easy to test. Along with all of our testing, we insisted that six criteria points be met before any part of the system could be considered a success.

1. The customers must be able to make a decision in less than 15 seconds on nine of 10 tests. This is because we observed while watching people shop in retail stores that customers had immediate access to good-, better-, and best-type shelves.

2. The customers must be very satisfied with their decision. Buyer's remorse must be minimal. This was easily tested. For example, they must not call back and complain that they paid too much. They must want to do business with us again the next time they need service. They must be willing and happy to refer us to their family and friends.

3. The customers must feel no sales pressure and exhibit no sales resistance at all. Our research had proven to us that sales resistance always came when the customers felt that someone was trying to sell them something. We also observed that when sales resistance was low, the buying patterns were incredibly predictable.

4. The technicians must feel no pressure to sell, upsell, or in any way manipulate the customer to buy more than they want to buy. This allowed the customers to feel safe with a quick decision.

5. The customers must buy more than just the bottom option on at least seven out of 10 visits.

6. There must be no price objection – at all.

Inspired by The Home Depot, we began to evaluate our own pricing as a contractor. Did we have a low-priced option for every service or sales call? What would happen if we did? We began to test this and found that we almost never lost a sale when there was a cheap option. Also, only 20%, or at the most 30%, of our clients would buy it. Everyone else would move up. After thousands of tests, we determined that every customer needed several choices on every decision, whether it was a task, a repair, or a piece of equipment, we settled on consistently giving five options every time.

Another key factor we needed to understand about the menu was where our lowest priced option should start. After all, have you noticed that your favorite hamburger place has had a 99-cent hamburger on every menu for the last five years, even though the price of hamburger goes up and down all the time? Your price is your power, remember? Pricing is powerful all by itself.

Knowing how fast the prices on the menu should rise and how high we could go with our top option were other details to factor in.

In the service world, the list of repairs can be very long. So when we set out to create our menu, we had to simplify this step. We started with what we called the 19 most common heating repairs and tested them in eight states. The success of these tests quickly led to over 700 different menus that would eventually include HVAC, plumbing, electrical, and equipment sales totaling our options on those menus to over 3,000 for the combined trades.

Seeking help from contractors around the country was our biggest asset. Matt and I took to the highways and began riding with the technicians to test our menus out in the field. It seemed that every day in homes and businesses generated weeks of work in the office. We tested and tweaked screenshots, pages, colors, bold-print prices, shaded paragraphs, formulas, and more. We even tested whether to use dollar signs beside numbers. Then we named our levels on the menu. We had many discussions over how to add value using option titles. We ran tests on consumer moods and reasons for needing the service call. There was a lot we needed to evaluate to produce the right system that would work the same every time.

IMPLEMENTATION AND CONSIDERATION

When we began the process of implementing this program for actual service companies, we learned quickly that there were four key areas we needed to concentrate on.

1. Customer retention.

    It was imperative that we paid close attention to the home/business owners who were getting the repairs. Contractors work very hard to get and retain customers. To jeopardize any of those relationships would have been very costly. And because online review sites like Angie's List and Yelp allow people to give immediate feedback, we needed to make sure the systems would not only be accepted, but liked by the general population.

2. The service technicians.

    If they indeed wanted no part in selling to customers, could we design the system to work in such a way that they enjoyed using it and would make their job easier? Could it also give them a more professional edge with the customers?

3. The office staff.

    These individuals have the day-to-day challenge of dealing with customers, from the very first phone call to scheduling and dispatching, collecting payment, and making sure they are happy enough to give of their business again. We asked ourselves, could our system work intuitively with the office staff, and could they begin to love the whole idea?

4. The owners of the company.

    Could a whole new selling system generate the kind of cash they always believed a company like this should generate? Could this make their job so enjoyable that they would wonder why they ever thought a service business was stressful in the past?

WHAT RESULTS DID WE NEED?

Money in the bank! This system had to bring in *big profits* for the contractors using our menu system. We wanted to cultivate out of our proven system debt-free companies that could fully enjoy the perks of success. They had to make money and, as the saying goes, work smarter, not harder. It was as simple as that. If it made their employees happier and their customers less likely to feel manipulated and overcharged, profit was inevitable, and we saw it immediately. And when I say profit, I mean contractors calling me and asking what they should invest in with all their extra cash!

We spent hundreds of hours testing, but once contractors began to use this system in various areas of the country, the testing became much easier. Eventually, we had clients using our methods in about 18 different parts of the country, and we began to revamp The New Flat Rate to try to get the customer to look up, then look down, then move up and choose. We tried different colors, words, fonts, and pricing formulas. Then success—we began to see consistency in the timing. Most customers were choosing an option in less than 20 seconds, so we worked, we tweaked, and we tested more, and now we have brought it down to 10 seconds.

Today, our system is used on service calls thousands of times every day, so we are now able to make thousands of tests of given phrases, words, headings, and even different colors. We keep testing because we believe constant testing brings constant improvement. Big companies constantly run tests. McDonald's tries out different menu boards all the time. And The Home Depot and Lowes keep running their tests. By continually evaluating stores like these and applying what we learn to our contracting business, we can quickly evaluate what will work for us and what will not. My good friend, author, and fellow consultant Jay Abraham said to me, "Rodney, your No. 1 asset is the ability to test, so test everything, and test it over and over." Your ability to test is your primary asset as well. So, as we say in the South, "Get crackin'."

Before menu pricing, my contracting businesses were strictly wholesale based. Our prices were set based on multipliers of the wholesale price of parts and equipment, then adding labor overhead and profit. We were pricing like the wholesalers we bought from. But I was set free from that old-school mentality!

Sure, we needed to know and respect what we paid for materials, but we found that the customers would pay much more if we sold something different from our wholesalers. We had something far more valuable that the customers would pay much more for—our expertise, our quality, our craftsmanship, and not to mention our experience. Even our tender loving care was found to have value. We discovered that for some services, the higher prices would be welcomed because it required a higher level of expertise. After all, that is what our servicemen want to do anyway, use more of their craftsmanship, skill, and talent, right?

It's easy to see what we as business owners and technicians want, but what is the process to make this change successful? An entire shift in your business model. You must believe that any attempt to sell results in increased sales resistance and objections, no questions asked. What we have learned is that business doesn't have to be a struggle! As my daughter, Melody, likes to say, "Everything is easier when sales double." And that at minimum is what our menu did then and is doing this very day. Why won't they pay me what I'm worth? They didn't know they could. Show them what you are worth and find a bank to hold your money.

Here's to You Getting Paid What You are Worth!

Rodney Koop

Founder/CEO

The New Flat Rate

Illustrations by Stephanie Koop

ABOUT THE AUTHOR

RODNEY KOOP

Growing up in rural Minnesota, Rodney began his career in the service industry at the ripe age of 15 when his father started him into an apprenticeship in the family's electrical business.

Over the last three decades, Koop has founded and sold HVAC, electrical, and plumbing service companies. Koop is a Master Electrician holding 12 unrestricted electrical licenses and has helped to write and qualify exam questions for state board testing. Rodney founded The New Flat Rate, the first in-home menu pricing system for HVAC, plumbing, and electrical contractors.

Rodney is also a motivational speaker, author, entrepreneur, and solutions-based enthusiast. He is dedicated to challenging all audiences to utilize their brains in creative ways for making life decisions and growing companies. Knowing fully what it's like to struggle in business, Rodney teaches companies how to rise from a foundation of strength, believing that success and advancement can be achieved with the right tools and expertise.

When he's not advancing his company, Koop can be found on the trails riding one of his four-wheelers, spending time with his nine children, or traveling around the world with his wife, Karen.

It's always about price until you make it about something else.

Rodney Koop